Pieces of Me

A Poetry Contemplation of my struggle with loss and healing.

Victoria Harrop

Dedicated to:

The memory of Austin Mondoux,
and our daughter Abigail Mondoux.

No one prepares you for the experience of death
Leaves you, raw, sore, put to the test
I wish I never felt this
Pure agony from the depths of my abyss
Forever ice shackled to my heart
knowing we will always be apart

Welcome to Pieces of me
From grief to the ability to see
I will always love this soul
Even when it's put out of my control

Is my life even real?
I thought I knew where it was going
The substances of the path that I was towing
I'm so angry, I'm hurt
I never knew life could be this low, in the dirt
I feel lost, I knew we aren't together, but I still care
I always wanted you there
First days, and last
You were never meant to become a past
I will forever make your name known
Even if you have gone
Your seed will know the love that you had
Even when battling the demons,
you had in your own head
She will know you were there, and you cared
I will forever save your voice for her
Share videos and photos, she will never, not know your
face
I want her to remember, every trace

I knew every detail, every pattern
I wish I could have spoken to you, a one last chance
Not mediocre, the real deep intense that we once shared
Just so I could shake you and have you here
Even though your vessel is no more
She will know you in the depths of her soul
For you will always be here
I will make sure she knows just how kind and caring a
daddy you were
My heart aches, I wish I could have done more
Now I am just left feeling punctured and sore
I will forever carry your name, in my heart, my mind, and
my soul, just like you would always say

Over a week has passed since I heard the news
Still feeling lost, on a nightmare cruise
The ship is going in circles
I'm still breathing, a small miracle
Eyes burning, heart churning
Restless, dried eyes
Angry with the way we said goodbye
Tossing, turning, I am sick
Working, pushing, getting the day over quick
Thoughts cascading, mind is racing
Items lost, I am misplacing
Questioning my beliefs
Not feeling any relief
Broken, trying, crying
Slowly parts of my soul are dying
....'Good morning mommy,' I hear
Waking me from the darkness, I steer
Start over again, my mind is starting to spin

The release of finally seeing you
Knowing that your fate is now true
Waves of emotions hit me
Tears stream down my face as I see
Your lifeless body does not breathe
It is making me break underneath
I just lay on your chest,
nothing but emptiness
A place where your once, heartbeat
Is now just as hard as stone, it seems
What is this deep inside that I'm feeling,
unease?
No heartbeat, I drop to my knees
Screaming in my head, wake up please!
Quiet

The day comes where everyone says goodbye
I feel hearts wrench, strangers, sigh
But they're not strangers, lives you've touched
I never heard a crowded room so hushed
I stand in line, with hugs and words to be given
Standing here in silence, in this position
How could you do this to me?
Leave me alone with our child of only three
This is not the road that I should have been on
We were supposed to co-parent, now I'm shaking
At the idea of you not seeing her grow
Now I feel nothing but low
Why do I feel this way?
How can I just escape?

Feeling the pull, of pressure
Struggling to find any pleasure
Forcing a smile, fooling the crowd
Trying not to be too loud
Looking at the pain I have done
To another soul, someone's son
It's ok, keep masking it
No need for discussion, blow up drinks are lit
Black out seems like the way
Uneasy, but it's okay
Flashes of my mind seem to go away
I am not living in reality
Pass out, What was last night's intake?

Waves of disgust portray my face
As I hear of last night's mistakes
I didn't mean to get lost in space
I'm sorry, please wake me, give me a shake
Share the news to the one by my side
Even though disagreements arise
I see the hurt cascade his face
Something that I personally cannot replace
Thinking I can do what it takes
I have been so lost since the wake

My thoughts have been scattered
I am lost thinking, shattered
I thought by now I would be able to mentally deal
But in reality, I am becoming toxic, it's unreal
Push away anything that has meaning
Like a baby on the bottle, to be weaning
Only have energy for my next of kin
Packing my emotions in the back of the bin
Thinking I have what it takes,
I am drowning in my own reality
Masking it with temporary amuses to my mentality
When will I feel like me again?
Is this the ending?

Can I sleep forever?
It is the space I can fully surrender
To the memories of you
From when we first met, to the time at the zoo
Living in guilt for feeling wrong
Thinking of how this hurt another,
I don't feel strong
Am I crazy for feeling any of this?
I hate the constant feeling of loss, and miss

Anger sweeps through the depths of my veins
Replaying every moment, in the remains
I hate this, I hate life
I want to quit
I keep going forward through the strife
I can't breathe, I'm suffocating
I'm struggling with communicating
Asking opinions, finding it everywhere else
Thinking its valid leaving welts
What's up, what's down?
By this point, I should have a red nose like a clown

I can't hear you anymore, where is my sign
My whole body has been out of line
I can't see straight, not even with glasses
I can't believe your body is nothing but ashes
It wasn't so bad when I could feel your presence
Now there's nothing, not even a hint of essence
Why am I so blocked?
What's the secret to become unlocked
I don't know any more
I am so far from myself, it's unfair
Should I dare?
To try and feel love again?
Is that the only time I will feel or see signs,
when I am Zen?

You ever feel like your continually falling
Not in a good way but in a way where you want to escape
To escape the thoughts that are controlling your mind
Escape the earth that holds you
Do you ever feel so broken that you can't piece yourself
back together again
Have you ever wondered where the happiness lies within
you
How to awaken it without feeling greedy
Do you know how it is to be compelled by the haunting
thoughts in your mind
But not act on them
Ever want to scream for help, but feel it's pointless
Ever want a hug, but feel like that makes you weak
Have you ever fallen down so hard that you can't seem to
bring your legs through the sand
It feels like quick sand slowly taking you in and suffocating
your every breath
Do you ever want to just close your eyes and not wake up.
Have you ever felt these thoughts but just kept going
Have you realized that your yourself are a warrior battling
your own war
Knowing that this is only the current state of the mission
but not the end of road

Did you know that being strong is more than just muscles
but also the capability to wake up
Have you opened your eyes that not everything is a fairy
tale
But a novel of deep despair, mystery, and love
Yet somehow your pages keep getting erased or ripped
out
Leaving you to rewrite your last chapter
Have you ever felt your soul rip out of your body
For reasons though you try to pull it back in.
During the emotional outbursts of tears, anger, and sleep
deprivation

Have you ever truly grieved that loss?
Only to realize it will always haunt you into a world of
acceptance for your pain
To only cry to yourself and in the privacy of your own
home just to try and put your make up on to go on
Will I ever truly feel alive again?

Wasting away at the seams
I can't eat, I can't remember my dreams
Pushing forward continuing through
Making sure I have something to pursue
Career? Love? Passion
Destroying all, like an assassin
I stopped caring for myself
Put it in a box on the back of the shelf
No, I can't continue to go like this
I have to resist
I am stronger than I perceive
I must open my mind to really see

I am healing
I am dealing
I have accepted the truth
For me and my youth
Even when some days are hard
I'm handling the deck of cards
I'll never truly understand life
To cut it deep with a knife
One day maybe it'll be clearer
As I look in the mirror
I want to grow, and water my home
Even on the days I'm left to roam
One step is all it'll take
To move my body and be awake

In all my darkness there's still a light
Even in the deepest of despairs
I know my greater purpose is just a threshold away
Continually pushing me to my limits
Never will I break
I will only get stronger

In every memory, there's a moment
One moment that made it light or dark
Currently I sit here and contemplate
The dark and the light
How I wish I knew how to feel like myself
How can I come back from this?
As I drag my boots,
I can feel the energy surge through me
The inner goddess in me, trying to break free
From the breaking of the loss
I will walk on water again
Until then, I will keep trying to swim

Todays the day, our young one grows older
Somehow I feel like there's a heavy boulder
Things I noticed you would handle
Are no more, as your photo hangs off the mantle
Trying my best to see the light shine through
As the children smile and laugh, a happy crew
I feel my heart ache, this is what we would share
Now I feel alone, even though your spirits here
In the sky, and the presence around
I suppose I'm just bitter that you're not on the ground
Next to us and our little soul of kin
I'll just have to continue to feel you within

More months keep passing and your gone
I thought that I be better but, I'm more withdrawn
Weeks are inching closer to Christmas
Trying to keep busy, minding my own business
I haven't had a drink in a solid time
Trying to stay in a clear state of mind
But emotions are over flowing me
Making my way, blurry, hard to see
Shopping for this holiday sort of speak
But I am not doing well, I am becoming weak
Everyone keeps repeating, 'first is the hardest'
Currently I am just trying to stay modest

The lights flicker on the tree
Houses are glowing with glee
My Christmas spirit feels at a loss
I'm trying my best through the thoughts
Smiling through this period
Hoping that my exterior
Doesn't truly show my hurt
I work with friends and family
Which keeps me grateful through the insanity
Just being kind to myself and others
Understanding under the covers
My brain isn't computing this tragedy
Wanting to form a strategy
It's my first Christmas since you are gone
I must say I feel with drawn
Our family reminds me of the love we share
Even when my heart is feeling bare
So I go on knowing this will be the first
Which will be the worst
As time goes on I can only see, how numb I will just be
Don't worry, I will keep on smiling, I will remember
Just breathe

Do you think I am smarter?
Kinder? Wiser?
Lately I have been struggling to be anything other
Currently sitting here, remembering the past
From the good to the bad, how it just went fast
Remembering how no matter what
I was what you wanted
You were persistent even when I pushed you away
Deep in my soul, I always wanted you to stay
I wish I would've known what I knew then
I would've tried to only let love in

HAPPY NEW YEAR!! The crowd roars
Couples kissing, I'm exiting doors
Hiding away, not wanting to be seen
For last year you were king and I your queen
We stayed in together, a happy family
Went to bed, felt stability
I still remember when midnight hit
You awoke me, that I'll admit
Just to kiss, and go back to sleep
Now I just sit here and weep
...these endless memories

I woke up today, not in a way you think
With some sort of glimmer of hope
I didn't feel like a constant sink
My heart still yearns and aches for you
I should probably stop hiding, seems overdue
I just need a sign of some true bliss
Where I know I can always feel happiness
It comes from within
Forever, a memory on my skin
Which will remind me to stay at ease
During the storms and the breeze
I just wish I could replay the true identity
Of who you were to me

Isolation seems ideal
As I am trying to fully heal
But is it? I am unsure as I groom myself through
Emotional well-being, to grow a new view
I am more
More loving, genuine, deep to my core
Disciplined, strength, positive
I am manifesting, becoming acquisitive
I am at the highest realm
A true leader, a true helm
I steer my ideas and belief
I am not hiding anymore, I have found relief

Lining up my chakras of pure intent
Even though I have wasted time spent
Working on the positive outlook
Re-writing chapters through the book
Knowing that each pain I have had
Will not define me, no matter how bad
I will progress to my truest form
As I am going through this storm

It's the little things that keep me afloat
From my daughters smile
To drifting in a boat
Sea sweeps, everlasting thought
Deep within me
I can't help but feel distraught
It'll be ok, not right now
But I can sense it in my soul somehow
Till then I will give my head a bow
As I glance at the goal

My heart hurts today
Knowing my birthday is approaching
But you're not here helping me through coaching
I don't feel positive about it
I'm trying to plan for myself, with friends
Everyone is busy, has life's, I understand
I just wish you could be here
Even when we weren't together, you made it special
I can't imagine another year without you
It's questionable

She cries for you,
How can I soothe something out of grasp?
It leaves me helpless and rasp
I don't understand how to make her better
Even when I give her your sweater
Nothing will be the same for her
You're gone, once were
The agony, I feel tears, rips my heart out
As I hear her cry, 'daddy,' I want to shout
Angry at you for having to make me battle
Sad with you, because of the shackle
On our hearts you left
Every little detail, every cleft
I wish we never had to live in this reign
Without you, it's too mundane

I dreamed about you, but not how I normally would
I was nothing but tears
I wept while you held me
I felt your hand on my face, wiped my tears
I remember feeling all my fears
I could feel the anger arise through me
As I tried to yell at you from all the history
Instead, I felt the warmth of your energy embrace
Then I had no face
Just the feeling of innocence
Our twin flame embrace

Another holiday is approaching
But I am keeping casual
Helping others. coaching
Mother's Day is just a couple of days away
Prepping baskets to bestow
Making sure your mom knows
How loved she is, even when we're both exposed
Holding my strength on the edge of my sleeve
To give gifts of light in seed
The end of the day has arrived
I soaked in the tub, knowing I survived

Healing is not what you expect
But it shows discipline, and self-respect
It's growth and isolation all at once
It can take days, weeks, even months
Slowly you will achieve your highest self
From that deck of cards, dealt
One day human form will make sense
Open your soul
Don't keep your mind dense

Trapped in the essence of my mind
Some thoughts persist to be unkind
Overwhelming, to say the least
Trying to cage the beast
Don't let it overtake me
Continue being in a sane reality
Shut eyes, deep breaths
Living this everlasting quest
I am the dragon

Shadow work is running through me
Knowing the little details, I couldn't see
Vibrating higher than I did before
Waiting for the takeoff, to soar
The universe guides me through this vessel
I am tired of a constant wrestle
Provide me with the undying knowledge needed
To overcome lessons, and feel defeat
Manifestation to my truest honor
I am genuinely starting to feel calmer

Messy, misplaced, a little impatient
I am beautiful
Understanding, caring, at ease
I am beautiful
Misheard, lost, and stubborn
I am beautiful
Graceful, kind, growing
I am beautiful
Wholeheartedly me, in all way
I accept the beauty within me.
I am more than what they see
Beauty is skin deep

Liquid drapes my cheek
As I sit in reminders
Missing your voice, hard to speak
All I wanted was to hear hello
Now I feel lonely and weak
Once I release the sadness in me
Continue with strength
A pivotal peak.

My pure soul essence is slowly revealing itself
Peace, serenity, love
All frequencies will bring me closer to indefinite wisdom of
thyself

Vibration running through the air
Surrounding me, intuition aware
Elevating to my strongest form
Making me distant from the norm
Breathing in the smell of pine from the tree
Beauty of nature is a guarantee
One day slowly, growing, and molding
Like clay forming rocks, bouldering
Hard, set in stone
Strength, mentally full grown
See me become a part of the rising sun
Dancing with the moon, I'm spun
Yin and Yang
I am all one

Father's Day is soon here
Seeing uplifting strength through the mirror
Planning my next steps
So, our daughter knows, and respects
That even though you're in heaven
We can send our love through proper expression
Floating hugs and kisses through a balloon
Letting it soar to the moon
Gifting your dad something extra special
As we coasted through another vessel

I'm elevated, fully concentrated
Ego not controlling direction
Never medicated
Feeling strength, connection
Still have days, frustrated
Sit through, full reflection
Growing can feel weighted
Universal protection
Hard shell can feel outdated
Break through, objection
Wings blooming through, elevated

Ever wonder what heaven is like?
I ponder the thought
Are there never-ending oceans, deep tides?
Are there clouds to rest your spirit upon?
Ever wonder the feeling of pure air
As it sweeps you up, no more despair
Do you ever wonder what heaven is like?
Closing my eyes, I dive into deeper psyche
Feeling waves of emotions surge
Wake up, let go, the purge
Knowing that one day, we all will know
What heaven is like, as we undergo

I see you in our daughter
eyes
She shares so many traits, I
realize
Artistic, loving, and stubborn
Dark sun kissed skin, never a
sunburn
Sweet, gentle, and full of
questions
Curious of life and all lessons
But parts of me seep through
Strength, beauty, persistence
to pursue
Energetic, voiceful of her

opinion
I can hear your voice, cheeks are crimson
Blessed beyond belief
Even as a feel this grief

Each day brings a new blessing
I see signs from heaven, is it you that's expressing?
Living in the idea of a new world
Bringing apparent, hurled
At me

It's almost a year since you're passing
I view everything differently, contrasting
Figuring out the pillar of each emotion
How to manage it easily without commotion
Provided new journeys, and someone new
Unexpected, is this overdue?

Grieving your life, never seems to end
I am not going to pretend
Opening has never been my strong suit
I usually become quiet and mute
Although this is not my way now
I figured out a way to express and endow
The benefit of it, our daughter needs to know
How to properly endure emotions, as she grows
One day at a time, I breathe deep
Our daughter's keeper speaks

I am feeling so grateful.
Everyone in my life is so helpful
I don't know how I could manage without friends and family
They help me keep my sanity
Helping me fall in love with my life again
Helping me become myself, with a spin
A spin of realization, pain, and sorrow
But knowing that there is always love, and tomorrow
Opening all this give and take
Knowing I have the strength and I won't break
As each moment passes, I still think of you
Knowing everything, and what I must do
You are forever a piece of me
No matter where the journey will take us, I won't forget
I will forever carry your name
For you have gifted me with life from our flame

ABOUT THE AUTHOR

Victoria is a young author that has been writing poetry since high school. She hopes that her words can inspire other people struggling with loss that they are not alone, and everyone does go through dark periods while grieving. Although there is darkness during these times, her writing helps elevate and push people into knowing that there eventually becomes a level of understanding to pursue the happiness within oneself and the beauty of life.